Spiritual Insights of T. W. Willingham

Book 5

Crumbs About the Humanity of Jesus

D0166578

Crumbs About the Humanity of Jesus

Beacon Hill Press of Kansas City
Kansas City, Missouri

Copyright 1987
by T. W. Willingham

ISBN: 083-411-1659

Printed in the
United States of America

Cover design: Crandall Vail

10   9   8   7   6   5   4   3   2   1

Contents

Foreword

Dr. T. W. Willingham is almost a legend in the Church of the Nazarene. He has served as pastor, district superintendent, college president, and executive at the world headquarters of the church.

Somewhat like Bernard Baruch he has been a close advisor to general superintendents and fledgling executive directors over the years. His business acumen and practical judgment have been sought after by all of us.

His greatest impact, however, has been in the spiritual realm. I and literally thousands have been stimulated by his insight into the Scriptures. Take these "crumbs," which I consider the most prophetic (prophetlike) pieces that have ever come from our presses, and revel in them.

—M. A. (BUD) LUNN

A Note of Thanks

First, I desire to thank my God for giving me time, strength, and guidance during the past 40 years as I have worked on the 16 books that I have had published.

In 1970, the Lord gave me a five-page directive concerning my writings in which He said, "I have given you two helpers . . . and it is My desire that they help you, and if they abide near Me they will feel the same way."

These two God-given workers—Clara Rogers and Kathy Butts—have been dependable and efficient and, more important, have felt that in so laboring they have been serving the Master and His kingdom.

Clara has corrected nearly all my handwritten articles, as well as typing many. Kathy has typed much, organized material, and by research and study, has made many valuable contributions. I thank God for both of them; without such help my work could not have been done.

If these messages prove to be of spiritual help to you, just give all the praise to our Heavenly Father.

—T. W. WILLINGHAM

Ye Shall Find an Ass Tied; and A Man Bearing a Pitcher of Water

The double caption of this chapter introduces two very interesting experiences in the history of Christ's last days upon earth.

The first, "Ye Shall Find an Ass Tied," introduces the story of Jesus' triumphal entry into Jerusalem and is recorded in the opening verses of the 21st chapter of Matthew, with some sidelights from Mark 11 and Luke 19.

The heart of this story is that Jesus foretold facts of the future and the actions of others well in advance of such acts.

Note some of them:

First: He gave definite instruction to His disciples as to where they were to go: "Go into the village over against you." There and there alone could they find the objects for which He was sending them, and an owner who would allow them to take them.

Second: He assured them that they would find immediately—no searching, no delay: "And straightway ye shall find."

Third: They were to find two animals, "an ass tied, and a colt with her," these two.

9

Fourth: He gave them an answer to give the owners, should they raise an objection. They did, and the answer was given: "The Lord hath need of them."

Fifth: The owners' favorable response would be immediate; no proof required, no surety bond to be posted, no haggling: "Straightway he will send them."

All five statements made by Jesus came to pass. They went into the next town "and found even as he had said unto them." "They . . . found the colt tied by the door without," in the open street. The owners "let them go"—a perfect fulfillment of Jesus' predictions.

The second half of our title—"A Man Bearing a Pitcher of Water"—introduces the story of the preparation for the Last Supper. The story is told in Matthew, chapter 26; Mark, chapter 14; and Luke, chapter 22.

Some have contended that there is nothing supernatural about this incident, that Jesus had already arranged with the landlord for this supper. But even if this should be assumed (which assumption we do not make), there are features in it that cannot be easily explained, so we take it as an illustration of superhuman knowledge and insight.

Note the instructions and results:

"Go into the city."

"There shall meet you a man bearing a pitcher of water."

"Follow him into the house where he entereth in."

Request the guest chamber there for the meal.

"He will shew you a large upper room furnished and prepared."

"His disciples . . . found as he had said unto them."

To meet the right man with the pitcher of water was not a mere accident; some knowledge more than human must have been at work here.

These instances, and especially the first, have been used

by some as proof of Christ's deity; however, they are no such proof.

Turn to 1 Samuel, chapter 10 for a parallel of superhuman knowledge—in fact, more pronounced than the two instances under consideration.

The prophet Samuel was conveying information to Saul of events yet to take place and of which the human mind, unaided, could have no knowledge.

Enumerate them:

1. "When thou are departed . . . thou shalt find two men"—no more, no less—*two*.

2. They will be "by Rachel's sepulchre."

3. "They will say unto thee, The asses . . . are found . . . thy father . . . sorroweth for you."

4. "Then . . . thou shalt come to the plain of Tabor, and there shall meet thee three men going up to . . . Bethel."

5. One will be "carrying three kids."

6. "Another . . . three loaves of bread."

7. "Another . . . a bottle of wine."

8. "They will . . . give thee two loaves of bread . . . receive."

9. Then "thou shalt come to the hill of God, where is the garrison of the Philistines."

10. "Thou shalt meet a company of prophets coming down."

11. They will have "a psaltery and a tabret, and a pipe, and a harp . . . they shall prophesy."

12. "The spirit of the Lord will come upon thee, and thou shalt prophesy . . . and shalt be turned into another man."

Other information and instruction was given to Saul, but the 12 items above could not have been accurately predicted by mere human knowledge. Samuel not only gave this array of detailed history in advance, but the record is: "All those signs came to pass that day." There are at least 15 separate

11

predictions made by Samuel involving a large number of people. They all came to pass. No accident here.

While Samuel foretold more future events here than Jesus did in the two instances above, we do not in any way argue that Samuel was divine because of this ability. He was a prophet in touch with a God who knows all things and can reveal them when and to whom He will.

Jesus, too, was a prophet and had access to God and claimed no such supernatural power as His own. His words are, "The Son can do nothing of himself, but what he seeth the Father do" (John 5:19). "I speak . . . those things which I have heard of him" (8:26).

A prophet, as Samuel, Jesus had contact with the Father and uttered His message. To claim that He acted with infinite wisdom and power while on earth is to belie His own statements and remove Him as a practical pattern for our life.

My Judgment Is Just

(John 5:30)

With all that we know and believe about this Man called Jesus, could anyone question His claim: "My judgment is just"?

The principle of justice had been established and practiced centuries before the coming of Christ. Of Abraham the Lord said, "I know him, that he will . . . do justice and judgment" (Gen. 18:19). Again it is of record that "David executed judgment and justice unto all his people" (2 Sam. 8:15).

Of God it is said, "Justice and judgment are the habitation of thy throne" (Ps. 89:14). Stephen, in his valedictory address, refers to the prophet's message concerning the birth of Christ as "the coming of the Just One" (Acts 7:52), and Ananias' message to the blinded Saul was that "God . . . hath chosen thee [to] . . . see that Just One" (22:14).

One could not expect less of the Son of God when, to His children, God said, "What doth the Lord require of thee, but to do justly, and to love mercy, and to walk humbly with thy God?" (Mic. 6:8). Christ came to "fulfil . . . the law" (Matt. 5:17), and we would expect Him to fulfill this requirement perfectly, which He did.

The question is not concerning His statement. We accept that as fact. He was just—just in His denunciation of the scribes and Pharisees, just in His appraisals of men's acts and motives, and He will be just to all mankind in the final day of judgment. All those things we firmly believe, but why do we thus believe? On what basis do we trust in His perfect judgment and justice?

Perhaps the immediate answer would be, He is the only begotten Son of God, and His justice is inherent in His Sonship. How could He be less than just and be God's Son? For many of my unthinking years this was the only answer that I required; in fact, no other was acceptable. This inadequate answer would have remained adequate but for the fact that He gave another answer, and His answers are always true and final.

Then, too, if His justice were an inherent quality, native only to His Sonship, how could we become just who have no such relationship with God? We need not go far for the answer. He answers it himself: "My judgment is just; because I seek not mine own will, but the will of the Father which hath sent me" (John 5:30).

He further clarified His meaning when He said, "My judgment is true: for I am not alone, but I and the Father that sent me" (8:16). His justice emanated from the Father. He did not stand alone, but by seeking the Father's will, He was able to reproduce the Father's qualities.

In this revelation of the Son's process, we discover a pattern for our own life. Jesus taught us to pray, "Thy will be done" (Matt. 6:10; Luke 11:2), but the necessity of doing so looms large when we are reminded that His life of justice sprang from such seeking.

When we conceive of His completeness as being native and inherent in His Sonship, we rule Him out as a pattern for our own life and mar the image of His perfect manhood that stands as a challenge for our emulation, and render of little value His statement, "I live by the Father" (John 6:57). He used this truth with telling effect in His first recorded encounter with the devil.

By attributing to the Master qualities that He obtained from the Father, we remove Him from the common path of

14

man and then find no footprints to follow. Just as the branch must abide in the vine to live and bear fruit, so the Son drew His life from the Father. He becomes a perfect pattern for us, and our helplessness need not defeat us, since we have access to the same Source of strength from which He drew His.

If His justice came from His seeking to know and do the Father's will and enabled Him to be just, by the same method may we fulfill His command to "do justly." There is no excuse for failure. His footstep lies before us, and His path leads us to the desired haven.

At first thought one hesitates to say that Jesus would not have been just in His own right, but that His justice came from His seeking His Father's will, although His statement clearly implies that to be true. Upon second thought we affirm that the source of His justice was not in himself but was derived from the Father, hence His seeking His will to obtain it.

We are encouraged to take this position because its parallel is clearly stated by Jesus himself. Of similar content were His words: "If I bear witness of myself, my witness is not true" (John 5:31). Thus speaking, He was affirming that apart from the Father, His record could not be relied upon. Only as His word corresponded with that of His Father could it be true. He thus recognized His Father as being the Source of all life, truth, and justice. Life itself and all of its qualities came from His Father. He lived by this Father. This He clearly affirmed. Severed from His Father, He would have been as the severed branch to be held for burning.

Such understanding of the Son does two things for us. It shows us plainly what Jesus often declared that what He had of life, love, and justice came from His Father; and it further points the way whereby we in our helplessness can draw from the same Source—love, life, justice, and power.

I Would Be Weak

I would be weak, "for when I am weak, then am I strong" (2 Cor. 12:10).

I am seeking to understand the weakness of God. All of my life I have heard of His power, and while I do not profess to fully understand His power, I seem to know more about His power than I know about His weakness.

In our efforts to get help from above, we often call upon the power of God to assist us. Never in my life have I heard anyone calling upon the weakness of God to assist him. We seem to feel that our problems are so great, and the forces of darkness arrayed against us are so powerful, that it would take the power of the infinite God to do us any good. In fact, sometimes—perhaps often—we think that even His infinite power would not be enough to aid us; or if aiding us, not enough to cause us to triumph.

It is written, "The weakness of God is stronger than men" (1 Cor. 1:25), so for the moment I am turning from a search for His power to an understanding of His weakness. His weakness is all that I need, so I pray, "Lord, let me be weak—as weak as Thy Son, Jesus Christ."

Just how weak did Jesus become? What was the earthly end of His weakness? Whatever it was, my desire is to share it with Him—share it in its entirety.

There can be nothing more glorious than to be like Jesus Christ—like Him in every attitude of soul, every purpose of life, every joy that He possessed, every sorrow that He endured, every suffering that He faced—even the death that He died. To be assured of His likeness in eternity, there must be a willing—in fact, enthusiastic—acceptance of His likeness in time. Death does not change the pattern of likeness; it but extends it. The suffering of time and the reigning of eternity are inseparably connected. "If we suffer, we shall also reign with him" (2 Tim. 2:12).

Just how weak did Jesus get? He got so weak that He died. "He was crucified through weakness" (2 Cor. 13:4). This is the weakness that I desire to more fully understand and, without reservation or hesitancy, share.

Jesus began His earthly career in utter weakness—a helpless Babe in a stable in Bethlehem. He was the Son of God then, as much so as when He was "brought forth; when there were no fountains abounding with water" (Prov. 8:24), or as He is now, seated at the right hand of the Father; but for His earthly sojourn He had emptied himself. He had come as a man to live among men. He had been rich, but He had become poor: "For ye know the grace of our Lord Jesus Christ, that, though he was rich, yet for your sakes he became poor, that ye through his poverty might be rich" (2 Cor. 8:9).

He did not come as poor, as some tell us, but He *became* poor, and one cannot be poor and rich at the same time. Likewise, He emptied himself of the superior knowledge and power that He had before coming to earth.

Some seem altogether unwilling to accept the fact that He emptied himself and became poor. To them He just *acted* like He had done so. To them, He was like a millionaire dressed in rags, with only 15 cents in his dirty clothes, leaning over a poor, sick, and starving man on his pallet of rags, and in pity turning his pockets wrong side out and sharing with the pauper his last three nickels—while all the time the money belt strapped around him carried 200 $20.00 bills.

Whatever the knowledge and power possessed by the only begotten Son before the Incarnation, He divested himself of it for His sojourn on earth. To think otherwise is to

17

repudiate all that He said of himself in this regard. He had become weak.

Note some of the weaknesses that He professed to have.

First: He was weak in *power:*

"The Son can do nothing of himself, but what he seeth the Father do" (John 5:19).

"I can of mine own self do nothing" (v. 30).

"I do nothing of myself; but as my Father hath taught me, I speak these things" (8:28).

"The Father that dwelleth in me, he doeth the works" (14:10).

If, as some affirm, Jesus had the infinite power and knowledge of God in another compartment of His being but carried it around under lock and key, why did He never pray to the God that He was, instead of to His Father in heaven? Nowhere do I remember seeing a record of His praying, "O infinite Christ that I am, give Me wisdom and strength." If He was the infinite One while on earth, why call upon another for help?

Then, too, why did He deny it and say that He could do nothing of himself?

The only answer to the whole question is the answer given by the apostle Paul, under inspiration of the Holy Spirit: "He emptied himself" (Phil. 2:7, margin). This not only makes sense, but it leaves me with full faith in the integrity of the Man that wore the seamless robe.

Second: He became weak in *possessions.*

I am painfully aware that I am poor. He comes to me and says, "I can understand you, for I too, am poor"; but should I be convinced that He had 200 $20.00 bills strapped around Him and had access to them, for in reality they were His own, then I would just forget the rest of His speech.

If, on the other hand, I could know that He was telling me the truth about His poverty, and then He should go ahead and explain that He was rich at one time but that He had laid it all aside and had left it with His Father and could only get it by calling upon His Father; and would further explain to me that His Father wanted to be my Father too, and if I should accept the Father's free offer of adoption, that I would thenceforth be one of the "heirs, . . . and joint-heirs" (Rom. 8:17) with Him and would have the same access to the Father, through Him—my Elder Brother—and in that partnership there was a promise that all my needs would be supplied "according to his riches in glory" (Phil. 4:19), then I could believe in His genuine poverty and His Father's available riches both for Him and for me.

Having become poor, and understanding the way to obtain the riches of the Father, He is able to unite with me and lead me into the storehouse from which He was drawing His full supplies. This empty Christ becomes my Companion in emptiness, that I might become His companion in fullness: "For your sakes he became poor, that ye through his poverty might be rich" (2 Cor. 8:9).

We become one in poverty, and by remaining one with Him, will share His eternal riches. Such a Christ I can understand and accept.

Third: He became weak in *knowledge.*

That He began as a child and grew up as a child, few will question. The same words used in telling of His early development were used in telling of the development of John the Baptist: "And the child grew, and waxed strong in spirit" (Luke 1:80; 2:40).

Some, accepting the necessity of development in His childhood, claim that He reached infinite knowledge and power later in life, perhaps at His baptism. It is this that we do not find in the Word of God.

The infinite in any realm where it may be applied—in knowledge, power, or otherwise—is like a universal stat-

19

ment. If it can be shown that there are exceptions, then the statement is not a universal statement. In like manner, if the power and wisdom of Christ was limited in any area, then they could not be infinite, as was the Father's. He affirmed such limitations, not in the days of His childhood but in the maturity of His ministry.

When His disciples inquired of Him the time of His return, Jesus answered: "But of that day and that hour knoweth no man, no, not the angels which are in heaven, neither the Son, but the Father" (Mark 13:32).

This announcement of knowledge was not before His baptism, but near the time of His death. If He did not know this—and that is His plain statement—then He was not infinite in knowledge.

When the disciples inquired as to the time that He would "restore again the kingdom to Israel," He answered, "It is not for you to know the times or the seasons, which the Father hath put in his own power" (Acts 1:7). Note that the Father alone knew this. When He indicated that this was in the Father's own power, He ruled out His power over it as He did in the reference above, quoted from Mark's Gospel.

On another occasion, when the sons of Zebedee came desiring prominent seats in the coming Kingdom, Jesus said, "But to sit on my right hand and on my left hand is not mine to give" (Mark 10:40). Here again, Jesus denied that He had the power to make these seat assignments.

These statements of limited power, limited possessions, and limited knowledge were made toward the end of His sojourn upon earth. In fact, the reference in Acts as to the time of the restoration of the kingdom of Israel was made after His resurrection, so we clearly see that He was not infinite while He was upon earth.

But why multiply arguments or bring forth more testimony from Christ? He stated plainly, "My Father is greater than I" (John 14:28). Can anyone be greater than the Infinite?

Jesus said that His Father was greater than He; it follows that the Son could not have been infinite while He was upon earth.

It is the ignorance, poverty, and helplessness of the Son of God that gives me hope and courage to seek to follow in His steps. The strides of an Infinite One do not fit my weak and faltering steps. If I follow the footprints to the gates of God, they must be those made by a man—"the man Christ Jesus" (1 Tim. 2:5).

Of the Son of God it was written that He was made "a little lower than the angels" (Heb. 2:7), for "in all things it behoved him to be made like unto his brethren" (v. 17), and "in that he himself hath suffered being tempted, he is able to succour them that are tempted" (v. 18).

Again we ask, "How weak did Jesus become?" The answer is written repeatedly in His own words. He became so weak that He could "do nothing" without the Father's help. Can one get weaker? This was the depth to which He condescended, and the utter helplessness that was His.

It is this weakness that I covet. Oh, to be weak—as weak as Christ, for weakness is the portal of strength. This is just another of the spiritual paradoxes announced by the Master. He taught that to be great, one must be servant of all. He taught that if one would go down, God would lift him up. He taught that if one would lose his life, he would save it. He taught that the harvest could only come by the death of the seed grain. Death becomes the gate to life. This is foolishness to the natural man, but it is the wisdom of God. There is no other way.

Our ignorance grows out of our own understanding. Therefore, it is said, "Lean not unto thine own understanding" (Prov. 3:5); and again, "If any man . . . seemeth to be wise in this world, let him become a fool, that he may be wise" (1 Cor. 3:18). "Where is the wise? . . . hath not God made foolish

21

the wisdom of this world? . . . God hath chosen the foolish things of the world to confound the wise" (1:20, 27).

The weakness that is to be desired is not an end within itself but the end of self and the beginning of a life "hid with Christ in God" (Col. 3:3).

Paul expressed it thus: "I am crucified with Christ: nevertheless I live; yet not I, but Christ liveth in me: and the life which I now live in the flesh I live by the faith of the Son of God" (Gal. 2:20).

He refers to the same in another way: "Whereunto I also labour, striving according to his working, which worketh in me mightily" (Col. 1:29).

Paul was speaking of the same thing that Jesus was talking about when He said, "The Father that dwelleth in me, he doeth the works" (John 14:10).

This same plateau of Christian living is spoken of in the Book of Hebrews: "There remaineth therefore a rest to the people of God. For he that is entered into his rest, he also hath ceased from his own works, as God did from his" (4:9-10).

The secret of such a relaxed life is abandonment to God, in which we allow Him to live His own life through us without interruption. The guiding principle of such a life is absolute obedience. There is no substitute for this law. It is the one law that Jesus announced for His own life when He came to earth, and the law He has laid down for all who would follow in His footsteps. The wisdom and strength of God will only be released to one who follows this law. All of the Christian life hinges on obedience. To fail here is to fail, period!

When one surrenders himself in absolute and eternal obedience to another, he is thereby confessing the superiority of the master to whom he is surrendering himself. Surrender is a confession of helplessness, and helplessness is the door to power and strength—the power and the strength of Another. It is at the end of ourselves that another life begins, for life begins with surrender.

Again we ask, How weak did Jesus become? He became so weak that He died. It was through this dark portal of death that He entered into the glories of the resurrected life. "Wherefore God also hath highly exalted him" (Phil. 2:9). This exaltation was a direct product of His voluntary condescension. The "wherefore" indicates that, and the whole teaching of Jesus confirms the principle.

What Shall I Say?

(John 12:27)

There are many things that I like about Jesus Christ. In fact, the better I come to know Him, the more I think of Him, and the nearer I feel to Him.

Nowhere do I come nearer to Him than when He allows me to see Him in His low moments, times when the human comes out in the open. I thank Him that He did not profess to be what He was not, and that I have found Him to be unlike much that I have heard of Him.

To know Him as He is is to know a man, tempted, tested, and tried as we are, a man of utter helplessness, depending upon the Father for everything and living a life of faith in the Father, as I must live.

The "What Shall I Say?" of our theme opens the door to one of His weak moments. He had come to "the lost sheep of the house of Israel" (Matt. 10:6; 15:24). He had gathered many of them to himself, but He had just remarked, "Other sheep I have . . . them also I must bring . . . and there shall be one fold, and one shepherd" (John 10:16). Even Caiaphas, the high priest, prophesied that Jesus "should gather together in one the children of God that were scattered abroad" (11:52).

Christ realized that the hour of His death was approaching: "The hour is come, that the Son of man should be glorified" (12:23). But one flock of sheep had not been reached; the Greeks were not in. Then comes the message that they were there inquiring for Him. This seems to be the final group to be gathered, and it signaled the end of His assigned task. The betrayal, the trial, the Cross, the final suffering loomed up before Him, and with His "soul troubled," He asked, "What shall I say?" (v. 27).

His first response was, "Father, save me from this hour"; but upon second thought, He answered himself, "But for this cause came I unto this hour." Here the set purpose of His life, twice announced—"Lo, I come . . . to do thy will" (Heb. 10:7, 9)—comes face-to-face with its execution. The flesh recoiled, but the soul arose and spoke the final word. It was not a new word. It was but the painful reaffirmation of the old, "Not my will, but thine, be done" (Luke 22:42).

His perplexing question gives courage and faith to me. I too have my "What shall I say?" moments, and a Christ who always knew just what to say could be of little encouragement to me in such moments of perplexity. I am glad that I do not serve a Christ who had all the answers when He was among men; at times He was asking the questions, and on other occasions He admitted that He had no answer. He always found the answers when He needed them and was content to let those go unanswered when the Father preferred not to tell Him the answers.

I am thrilled to know that I have such a Christ—One who didn't know everything and who couldn't do everything. He did point the way to a Father who could give us all the power and the knowledge that we need, and He was content to ask no more. His prayer was ever in the spirit of "Not my will, but thine, be done."

Even in this dark hour, He prayed, "Father, glorify thy name" (John 12:28). He knew full well what was in this glorifying of the Father. It meant that He, the "corn of wheat," must "fall into the ground and die" (v. 24). He knew that He must be "lifted up from the earth" or He could not "draw all men" unto himself (v. 32).

The very perplexity of His soul encourages me, for I get perplexed almost beyond measure; but I do not despair, for my Elder Brother walked through these serpent-infested

25

marshes and left the markings of His trail behind Him. I see Him standing at the Father's right hand, beckoning Stephen home; and I know that by following His path, I, too, can be united with Him at last.

The weakness of Christ inspires me. His lack of knowledge encourages me; His hours of darkness bring hope when my soul seems lost in the fog; His ever-present "Not my will, but thine" stands as the immovable foundation upon which I, too, can stand.

When in this dark hour (one of the darkest) He made His perplexing cry, He was not left alone. "Then came there a voice"; the heavens were not silent: "I have . . . glorified it" was the response. The Father had been glorified in the Son's obedience, and with this response there came a promise: "I . . . will glorify it again."

What a heartening message this must have been to the suffering Son! It was an expression of confidence that the fidelity of the Son would continue and that the Father would receive further honor for himself.

Jesus was strong enough to reveal His weakness, and weak enough to be an encouragement to His followers. We praise Him now, 2,000 years later, not only for the fact that He took upon himself the form of man and was made "in all points" like unto us (Heb. 4:15), but we thank Him because He did not hide His true nature from us. When He showed His disciples the nail prints in His hands and feet, they knew that it was He. By the same token we know that He is bone of our bone and flesh of our flesh when He shows us the struggles of His soul, the limitations of His life, and His constant faith in His Father.

At no time does Christ rise higher than when He stoops the lowest, and at no point does His love appear more alive than in His death. Thus acting and living, He points the way for us by the path He has already taken. To follow is to find Him in glory.

Jesus Followed the Devil

It is shocking to think, and more shocking to write it down, that Jesus followed the devil. As shocking as it seems, the fact remains: He did.

Look at the words of Matthew: "Then the devil taketh him up into the holy city, and setteth him on a pinnacle of the temple" (Matt. 4:5).

Matthew continues, "Again, the devil taketh him up into an exceeding high mountain, and sheweth him all the kingdoms of the world" (v. 8). If He did not follow the devil, how could the devil take Him? And if He was not taken, how could the devil show Him the kingdoms of the world from that vantage ground, if He had not gone along?

Someone objects that this was but a mental picture and not a physical taking. Even if Christ went in mental process, He did not blot the scene out by refusing to think on it. From any viewpoint, the fact remains: Jesus followed the devil; either in body or in mind, He went along.

As horrible as these facts appear at first thought, they open up a facet of the Master's life too long unviewed by some. It was in the area of temptation that He invited us not to follow Him. "Follow me" was His general invitation, but when it came to the area of temptation, He posted the sign, "Follow me not."

This is implicit in the prayer He taught us to pray: "Lead us not into temptation" (Matt. 6:13; Luke 11:4). The Spirit led Him into the very jaws of the tempter. It was necessary for Him to know the full strength of the seducer. He must follow

27

him into all of his hiding places; and before going back to the Father as the world's Redeemer, He must explore the enemy's last stronghold, even death and hell.

Like Paul, we get acquainted with many of Satan's devices as we journey the upward way and meet him on life's many battlefields, but all of them we will never know. However, the Son must know all of ours and some that were peculiar to Him alone; hence, He followed the devil to his devilish worst. He must meet him on the throne of his power and conquer him completely. This He did.

Since Christ taught us to pray that the Father would lead us not into temptation, it is our duty to shun that which we have asked the Father to keep us out of.

From the very beginning, the devil has seduced people into sin under the guise of advanced knowledge. To the first pair, he said, Disobey and eat, and you will be like God, to know both good and evil.

It sounded so wonderful, just to be like God—to know the whole and not just a part. They ate and came to know, and from that disobedience sin has left its blight upon man, beast, and all else of earth, and has made the whole creation to travail in pain, waiting for the redemption of the world.

This temptation of Adam and its resulting sin haunts us every moment. Youth wants to know the thrills of life, be they legitimate or otherwise. Even grown people often go to questionable places and participate in questionable practices, that they may know firsthand, so they say, just what men of the world face. The lure often works, and sin slays another victim. Let Christ explore the enemy's camp and tell us how to overcome him.

Perhaps an equally important thing was done in Christ's following the devil. Satan had deceived the first Adam, and through him he had swept the whole race from the narrow path of obedience. He must have been self-confident, believing he could deceive the "last Adam" also. Satan must be given that opportunity. Christ must not be triumphant by bypassing Satan's traps but by passing through them. Of Him it is said, "that through death he might destroy him that had the power of death" (Heb. 2:14). Note, it was not by evasion but by experiencing death that He became its conqueror.

In like manner, He followed the devil into all of his traps, explored all of his devices, experienced his death, passed through his hell, and conquered at every point. The enemy has no untried scheme or unknown device or power that Christ did not meet; hence Christ can say, "I have overcome the world" (John 16:33).

Christ knows the seductive power of every satanic offer and every tinseled trap set for unstable souls. He knows also the amount of testing that each of us can take and the strength of each test, and has promised that the weight of the test cannot exceed our ability to bear. Hence victory may be ours always.

Thus Christ learned from His full exploration of Satan's domain just how to help us to overcome in every conceivable temptation and trial. He "was in all points tempted like as we are" (Heb. 4:15) and knows how to help us to meet them and be victorious.

With such a view of Christ, who thus willingly suffered for us and has gladly "borne our griefs, and carried our sorrows" (Isa. 53:4), and is still interceding for us, how can we do less than fall at His feet in total dedication and give Him our all forever and forever. I do! Do you?

This Man Never Learned

Jesus had been teaching in the Temple, "and the Jews marvelled, saying, How knoweth this man letters, having never learned?" (John 7:15). Thus speaking, they frankly admitted that He knew, and that His knowledge came not from the school of men; their very question showed that they were ignorant of His teacher and the school in which He was a pupil.

Jesus' understanding of spiritual truth and the written Word had been well established. It came to light first when, as a lad in the Temple, He both asked and answered questions. The scribes "were astonished at his understanding and answers" (Luke 2:47).

Early in His ministry Jesus "put the Sadducees to silence," and the multitudes "were astonished at his doctrine" (Matt. 7:28). "When the Pharisees had heard that he had put the Sadducees to silence, . . . a lawyer, asked him a question, tempting him" (22:34-35). Jesus answered from the Word, and there was silence.

On another occasion "a certain lawyer stood up, and tempted him, saying, Master, what shall I do to inherit eternal life?" (Luke 10:25). Jesus quoted the first and second commandments to him, but he still sought to justify himself and to entangle Jesus on the meaning of the word "neighbour." He probably knew that Jesus was not a "scholar"; and since he was, he could (as he thought) confuse Jesus by his scholarship. Jesus set the trap, and the lawyer walked in and was caught!

Another group that had been sent to entrap Jesus returned, admitting, "Never man spake like this man" (John 7:46). He silenced all who challenged Him, and at the end of every encounter it could be said, "They could not answer him again to these things" (Luke 14:6).

Finally, the religious teachers gave up: "Neither durst any man from that day forth ask him any more questions" (Matt. 22:46). Jesus stood in the arena alone, unchallenged but rejected. His "letters" could not be denied, His logic could not be answered, His word could not be broken. It stood in the majesty of truth, truth that abides forever.

The humiliating thing to the Jews was the fact that this admitted and fully demonstrated wisdom and understanding did not come from their schools. Their whole intellectual system was being devalued. Their traditions had been openly challenged, and they were unable to defend them.

Since they had come face-to-face with a mouth and wisdom that they could not answer, to allow it to continue would upset their seats of authority; there was but one course that they could take if they were to save themselves, and that they took: They "sought to kill him" (John 7:1)—and did.

The lamentable thing about this whole affair is that these Jewish teachers knew nothing of any source of spiritual knowledge but their own schools; hence Jesus was an enigma to them—the source of His knowledge unknown. They had the dead letter of the law but no contact with its Author.

Paul describes their condition thus: "For they that dwell at Jerusalem, and their rulers, because they knew him not, nor yet the voices of the prophets which are read every sabbath day, they have fulfilled them in condemning him" (Acts 13:27).

Jesus had told them that He had received His doctrine from God, but since they did not know Him nor the school that He attended, the source of Jesus' wisdom was unknowable to them.

Jesus reminded them that "it is written in the prophets, And they shall be all taught of God" (John 6:45). This the Jews should have known, but they knew not the voices of the prophets. They had built around the laws that had been God-given a vast network of traditions and had themselves become the final authority on matters religious.

The scribes and lawyers considered themselves the final word on matters religious and could accept no other source of truth but themselves. The God of Moses had spoken once and then ceased to speak! They had no contact with God and refused to believe that anyone else could have. To them Jesus was a blasphemer because He claimed such contact, and His death was justly due.

This danger of settling for a "God that was" instead of a God that is, has ever been with us. We have been warned, "Take heed, brethren, lest there be in any of you an evil heart of unbelief, in departing from the living God" (Heb. 3:12).

Men have a god—always have had and always will have. "There be gods many," Paul tells us (1 Cor. 8:5). The danger is not that we will give up a god, but that we will give up God, the "living God," the God that can speak, for His speaking is a proof that He is living. When the psalm writer wanted to indicate false gods—idols—he described them: "They have mouths, but they speak not: eyes have they, but they see not" (Ps. 115:5).

When one departs from the living God, he comes to rely upon the "best thinking of good men." His standard of judgment is "scholarship"; the Ph.D. becomes the symbol of authority, and but little attention is paid to the Word and almost none to the speaking Spirit.

It is difficult to have great scholarship and deep spirituality, just as it is difficult to have great riches and deep piety. It is possible, Jesus tells us, but rare. "How hardly" shall the rich and the highly educated enter into the narrow way. Not many rich will be saved, and "not many wise . . . are called" (1 Cor. 1:26).

It is distressing that in the face of the heavenly warnings there is a clamor for worldly wisdom and riches to the almost universal neglect of the spiritual. Many seem willing, in fact, anxious, to take the risk. Rank and praise of men are powerful forces. The "deceitfulness of riches" (Matt. 13:22; Mark 4:19) has trapped many a soul, and prestige of knowledge has cooled many a burning heart. Be warned now.

Buried with Him . . . Risen with Him

(Col. 2:12)

"Buried" and "risen"—two extremes; life and death brought together in one person. The death and resurrection of our Lord forms the pattern for us; to be like Him, we must share these two experiences with Him.

To understand the nature of the death that is required of us in order that we may have the resurrection promised to us, we need to understand the death of Christ, which is the pattern for us. We must be united with Him in His death before we can join Him in His resurrection.

We shall begin to look into the life of Christ at the point where He was "made . . . sin" (2 Cor. 5:21), for it is at this point, and here alone, that Christ and the sinner first meet. He came to man's sinful level, being made sin himself, that He might be united with sinful man for the ordeal of dying a sinner's death.

The sinner must be "buried . . . in the likeness of his death" (Rom. 6:4-5), else there can be no resurrection with Him. The action must be a joint action all the way through. For this reason man should understand the death of Christ. His was an hour of desertion; God left Him to suffer the consequences of sin. The whole punishment of man's sin must be met by Him, for He had assumed the debt, thereby making it His own. The total and final helplessness of Christ was reached in the hour of His total death. In His life, He had

34

said, "I can of mine own self do nothing" (John 5:30); and in total completeness could this be repeated while He was in the regions of the damned. He had no power of His own by which He could extricate himself. He must be raised, if raised at all, by the power of God. He did have a promise that power would be extended to Him for that Resurrection. He said, "This commandment have I received" (10:18). His own helplessness was complete; His sole hope was in Another.

If the sinner, "dead in trespasses and sins" (Eph. 2:1), is to be resurrected into "newness of life," he must be "planted together in the likeness of his death" (Rom. 6:4-5). He must come to the point of utter helplessness—"having no hope, and without God" (Eph. 2:12). He must realize that he is utterly dependent upon Another for deliverance. He must dash into the flames all hopes of life based upon his own goodness, and resign himself to the agonies of eternal death, unless Another rescues him from death. He must accept his plight as being just and his deliverance, if any, an act of pure and unmerited mercy. His death must be real, and his helplessness complete. He must find his oneness with Christ in this dark hour of despair and realize that they are both suffering, he justly for the sins he had committed, and Christ for the sin that He had made His own. I believe that here the sinner and Christ become united, bound by the cords of a just punishment. It is this complete and total unity in death that makes possible unity in the resurrection. To be with Him in death is to be with Him in life.

Christ was to accept this union with sinful man. This was in the cup that He asked God to let pass, but seeing that it was the only way that redemption could be had, He bowed His head and said, "Nevertheless not my will, but thine, be done" (Luke 22:42).

Man's sin had to become His own that the punishment might be just; herein lies the secret of our being justly forgiven. Unless Christ justly suffered, how could we be justly forgiven? If He had not made our sin His own, our redemption would have remained forever an act of mercy; but since He suffered justly, it can be said, "If we confess our sins, he is faithful and just to forgive us our sins" (1 John 1:9). We are forgiven justly because He suffered justly.

This truth is not in conflict with Peter's statement that "Christ also hath once suffered for sins, the just for the unjust" (1 Pet. 3:18), and that He presented himself as "a lamb without blemish and without spot" (1:19), and the further statement that He "offered himself without spot to God" (Heb. 9:14).

The picture here is the lamb brought for the sacrifice: It must be spotless. It was just that it should live; it had done no wrong, had no disease, and was spotless; but when it was placed as a substitute for sin, its death was just.

Christ must needs be pure, holy, without spot, and blameless; thus He must present himself as a sacrifice for sin. This He did, but the sin of the world must be dealt with not "by" Christ, but "in" Christ. He himself must become the embodiment of sin, "who . . . bare our sins in his own body on the tree" (1 Pet. 2:24).

The very argument that Paul uses for our being made righteous is that He was made sin. "For he hath made him to be sin for us . . . that we might be made the righteousness of God in him" (2 Cor. 5:21). We claim to have received actual (not imputed) righteousness—a righteousness that is real; and how could a real righteousness come to us if He was not really made sin? The reality of the one must rise or fall with the reality of the other.

The sinner now having fully identified himself with Christ in a just death, shares with Him in the Resurrection. When God raised Christ, He raised all who were in Christ. Both were raised by the power of God, and the sinner now enjoys a peace with the risen Son in the heavenlies. Having been buried together, they are now risen together. It is the acceptance of the just death and the oneness with Christ in death that guarantees the Resurrection power.

The debt of sin has been fully paid, and all who thus unite with Christ in this death process are freed from sin—justified freely through the complete payment of the debt of sin by Christ and the acceptance thereof by a living faith. Truly "buried," we are truly "risen."

Lazarus Is Dead.
And I Am Glad

The 11th chapter of John's Gospel has the story of the sickness, death, and resurrection of Lazarus. We would examine only one item in this interesting story, the statement of Jesus to His disciples that Lazarus was dead. This announcement by our Lord, before word was received of Lazarus' death, has been used by some to show His divine nature.

The message came to Jesus and His disciples while they were "beyond Jordan . . . where John baptized": "Lord, . . . he whom thou lovest is sick" (John 11:3). Jesus said to His disciples, "This sickness is not unto death, but . . . that the Son of God might be glorified" (v. 4). Whereupon "he abode two days . . . where he was" (v. 6).

Jesus then said to His disciples, "Our friend Lazarus sleepeth; but I go, that I may awake him" (v. 11). The disciples, misunderstanding Christ's meaning of sleep, were told "plainly, Lazarus is dead" (v. 14).

Apparently they had received no word of Lazarus' death before they started for Bethany; hence Jesus' announcement is held as a proof of His deity.

The whole story indicates that there was something very special to come from this miracle. Note some of the facts that indicate it. Above, we have noted that Jesus said this temporary death was to bring glory to himself. Note, too, that He lingered two days before starting. Again, note that Jesus stated that this delay, to give undeniable certainty to Lazarus' death, would set the atmosphere to create faith in the disciples when Lazarus was raised.

To add to all else, the prayer of Jesus at the grave is significant. He prayed, "Father, I thank thee that thou hast heard me" (v. 41). He offered prayer not that He might get an answer—He had that already—"but because of the people . . . I said it" (v. 42).

There is no question about Lazarus being dead. Jesus announced that "plainly" before leaving for Bethany, and again it is written, "He that was dead came forth" (v. 44). Those that buried him and the Jews that came down from Jerusalem believed this. Martha was sure he was dead, for he had been buried four days and "by this time he stinketh" (v. 39).

The story seems to add up to this: Jesus knew that Lazarus was dead before leaving for Bethany. He knew that this was to strengthen the faith of His followers and bring honor to God and to Him. He had talked this over with the Father and knew what to do, and when to do it, and the purpose of the doing. This could explain the delay of two days. It was before starting that He received directions and an answer to His prayer.

He had seen the Father's hand stretched out to raise Lazarus, and He acted as the Father's visible Agent, as He had been doing. This is evident, for He had said, "The Son can do nothing of himself, but what he seeth the Father do" (John 5:19). He had the mind of the Father and executed it.

Our main purpose here is to show that the prior knowledge of Lazarus' death cannot be used to prove that He was divine. He did have knowledge above the human—that is evident; but it does not follow that this supernatural knowledge arose from an inherent deity. The miraculous pre-knowledge is evident; its source is the only question.

Raising a dead man to life does not involve the free moral agency of man. It is wholly subject to the power of

God; and since that is true, God could raise Lazarus at His will and could announce His purpose to do so in advance.

Jesus said that it is the work of the Holy Spirit to "shew you things to come" (John 16:13); and an Old Testament seer tells us, "Surely the Lord God will do nothing, but he revealeth his secret unto his servants the prophets" (Amos 3:7).

The miraculous things that are found in this story have parallels in God's dealings with His prophets, and it is nothing strange that He should deal thus with His Son. In Old Testament times "women received their dead raised to life again" (Heb. 11:35); Peter raised Dorcas from the dead. Many times God told His prophets what was going on in other places and in the minds of others. God's prophet told Ahab of his death and where the dogs would lick his blood. The Lord revealed David's sin to the prophet. God promised Abraham a son by Sarah; He promised Hezekiah 15 additional years, foretold famines, promised deliverance of Israel from Egypt 400 years in advance.

In short, God has been foretelling events for thousands of years, revealing secrets to Daniel and a score of others, and can tell anything that He knows, within His power to perform, to anyone at any time He so chooses.

What Jesus foreknew and what He did in this story do not necessarily prove His deity anymore than that deity was proven in apostles and prophets in other similar cases.

These facts in no wise detract from His Sonship, nor do they fade the luster of His crown. Truth does not injure the faith or the character of anyone, and neither God the Father nor His only begotten Son are thrown in bad light by telling the truth concerning them.

We have been wreathing a halo about the brow of the Son for so long that we have failed to see Him as He said himself to be: "in all things . . . made like unto his brethren" (Heb. 2:17). Too often, He is worshiped in awe and distant wonder as a holy idol—untouchable, unapproachable, and unfollowable.

It is the picture of the Christ waiting upon the Father for guidance and understanding—helpless without the Father's help, ignorant without the Father's wisdom, and living always by the Father—that opens the way for us to follow Him. He was on our level, not above us, understanding us through himself.

41

Christ Never Had
All the Answers

The caption of this chapter is not a reflection on the only begotten Son of God—my Lord and my Savior. He announced that He was the Way, the Truth, and the Life, and He dealt always in truth—truth about the Father, about the devil, about those to whom He ministered, and the truth about himself. He who was the essence of truth could not be defamed but only honored by the truth concerning himself, and the truth is that He never had all the answers.

Evidently His disciples were of that school of thought whose slogan was "Christ has the answers—all the answers," and were probably shocked when they learned that their Master was not the all-knowing God, but the only begotten Son of the all-knowing God, and did not possess all knowledge himself.

They were anxious for answers that they did not need to have. Their curiosity carried them too far, and Jesus told them frankly, "It is not for you to know the times or the seasons, which the Father hath put in his own power" (Acts 1:7). When He reminded them that the Father had put this knowledge in His own power, He was but reaffirming the fact that the Father had not shared this knowledge with the Son. This fact they should have known, for earlier He had told them plainly, when speaking of His return, that "of that day and that hour knoweth no man, no, not the angels which are in heaven, neither the Son, but the Father" (Mark 13:32). They may have accepted this last statement as being true at the time it was spoken, while their later query was made after His resurrection, and surely by that time He should have known.

They could have been of that group of theologians who have clouded His humanity and demanded that He be equal with the Father in all things, or else their immortal and important souls could not be redeemed by one less knowing. They have insisted that although He was a crying, helpless babe to begin with, somewhere along the line He reassumed His original status, of which He had emptied himself, and was now equal with the Father in all things. True, the school is divided on just when this happened; some say it was at the age of 12 when He was asking and hearing questions in the Temple; some say it was when He was baptized in Jordan; some say it was when, after His wilderness temptation, he "returned in the power of the Spirit into Galilee" (Luke 4:14); while others say it was when the Father raised Him from the dead and had Peter to announce, "Therefore let all the house of Israel know assuredly, that God hath made that same Jesus, whom ye have crucified, both Lord and Christ" (Acts 2:36).

While there is no agreement among them as to when it happened, those of this school affirm that it had to happen— He must be equal with the Almighty, for they could not entrust their valuable souls to one so inferior! Like Naaman, they disdain the message of the "servant" sent of God and will listen to no one but the Highest.

It is amusing to see this wonderful spirit of Lucifer rearing its head and again demanding equality with the Almighty—the very demand that the Son refused to make. I know of no place in the Word of God that we are promised equality with the Father, either now or hereafter; but it has been written, "We shall be like him [the Son]; for we shall see him as he is" (1 John 3:2). Those who have already self-determined that the Son and the Father are equal in every

43

respect believe that since the promise, when fulfilled, will make us like the Son (and He is like the Father), we will then be as the Father, for two things equal to the same thing are equal to each other. Thus the ambition of Lucifer is realized by the "holy"!

I have often wondered why those who demand that the Son be equal with the Father defend their position with such fever—ever denouncing anyone who dares to question their sacred position. It is clearer now. Fever is caused by infection; and when one declares Christ to be equal with the Father in power and knowledge, he has a fever-producing infection and should get rid of the disease.

How may this be done? Just face the truth about Jesus as He gave it to us. He told James and John that He did not have the power to seat them by His side in the heavenlies. The Father had reserved that power to himself and had not shared it with the Son. Likewise, the Father had veiled the time of the Son's return from Him. Thus the Son was limited in both power and knowledge.

The relationship between the Father and the Son is more clearly illustrated: Cf. Matt. 22:44; 1 Cor. 11:3; 15:24-28.

The Father asked the Son to sit by His side until He (the Father) put all things under the Son's feet. Jesus, with His helpers, will then reign and rule "with a rod of iron" for 1,000 years (Rev. 19:15; 20:4).

"Then cometh the end," and Jesus will hand the Kingdom back to the Father. "And when all things shall be subdued unto him, then shall the Son also himself be subject unto him that put all things under him, that God may be all in all" (1 Cor. 15:24, 28).

Jesus was always obedient to the Father while on earth, and here it is revealed that throughout all eternity the Son will be "subject" to the Father—a position that Lucifer refused to accept.

44

Jesus Did; I Don't

The very title of this chapter—"Jesus Did; I Don't"—disturbs me. It is well that it does, for no message will be challenging to the reader that was not first challenging to the author. One cannot convey to others what he does not possess. "Such as I have give I thee," spoken by Peter to the lame man at Jerusalem's Temple gate (Acts 3:6), is a law of life universal in application. Regardless of how one may strive to give that which he does not have and to be other than his true self, the strain of thus living *will* ultimately appear, and under the pressures of life the hypocrisy will be revealed.

The only way to live a happy, carefree life is to live it from a holy center, where transparency is not painful and the light of truth is always welcome.

O God, may I have honesty of soul in developing this subject, and may the same honesty characterize any who may peruse it.

There are some things that Jesus did that I can never do, and some experiences that He had that I can never have—some that I do not desire to have, for in some of life's roles He stands removed and alone. I have no desire to walk in all of His footsteps; in fact, I should not. That is what He said, and He knows best.

It may appear to be double-talk for one to lustily sing, "Oh, to be like Thee! blessed Redeemer," and in the next breath declare that he has no desire to walk all the way with Christ. The sentiment of the song is relative; my statement is absolute. Speaking in a general way, I want to be like Him;

"This is my constant longing and prayer." I do not change that desire and prayer. I just don't apply it to all that Christ did. I should not.

To illustrate what I am saying: When Jesus entered Gethsemane, He "saith unto the disciples, Sit ye here, while I go and pray yonder" (Matt. 26:36). Then He took with Him Peter, James, and John and went deeper into the garden. Leaving them with the words "Tarry ye here, and watch with me," He "went a little farther" (vv. 37-39). The Good Shepherd has always gone before the sheep. The depth of that agony can never be fully known by man. I agree with the author of the hymn "The Ninety and Nine":

> But none of the ransomed ever knew
> > How deep were the waters crossed,
> Or how dark was the night that the Lord passed through,
> > Ere He found His sheep that was lost.

We may have our so-called Gethsemanes and may in a measure share His suffering for sinful men; but He, and He alone, did "taste death for every man" (Heb. 2:9); He, and He alone, could bear the sin of "the whole world" (1 John 2:2). If the weight of one lost soul upon the intercessor's heart is crushing, then what must have been His agony when He drank the cup for all? To this depth no mortal man can go. Only the Son of Man could plumb it, and He must do it alone.

Isaiah envisioned this centuries ago and expressed the thought of the Savior thus: "I have trodden the winepress alone; and of the people there was none with me . . . I looked, and there was none to help; and I wondered that there was none to uphold" (63:3, 5). In lone Gethsemane He did look, "and findeth them asleep." There He "wondered" and lamented, "What, could ye not watch with me one hour?" (Matt. 26:40).

He must go this path of redemption alone. Sinful man could not bear his own sin, much less the sin of others, therefore "the Lord hath laid on him the iniquity of us all" (Isa. 53:6).

At the periphery of His living the multitudes thronged Him; at the center He stood alone. He sent the multitudes away; then "he was there alone" (Matt. 14:22-23).

When the populace was demanding that He be made king, "he departed again into a mountain himself alone" (John 6:15).

When the glory of the Mount of Transfiguration had faded "and when the voice was past," and the two heavenly messengers (Moses and Elias) had returned, "Jesus was found alone" (Luke 9:36).

When the pressing throng was melting away, Jesus asked the Twelve, "Will ye also go away?" (John 6:67). They remained for a while, but in the end "the scriptures must be fulfilled. And they all forsook him, and fled" (Mark 14:49-50). The decree of divine judgment had already been pronounced against the Redeemer, and Jesus reminded them that "it is written, I will smite the shepherd, and the sheep . . . shall be scattered" (Matt. 26:31). He knew and was frank to tell them, "All ye shall be offended because of me this night." He must go beyond; He must stand alone; all men must and did forsake Him. He must go "without the camp" (Heb. 13:11).

Having affirmed that "ye shall be scattered . . . and shall leave me alone," He hastened to add, "And yet I am not alone, because the Father is with me" (John 16:32). He was still within that promise, "When my father and my mother forsake me, then the Lord will take me up" (Ps. 27:10).

His hour of total aloneness had not yet come, but it was on its way. Though mankind had forsaken Him, His Heavenly Father had not.

Although His followers of that day did forsake Him, the Pentecostal enduement of the Holy Spirit would enable His children to follow Him in total rejection by mankind but with

His abiding presence. His promise was "I will never leave thee, nor forsake thee" (Heb. 13:5); "Lo, I am with you alway, even unto the end of the world" (Matt. 28:20). To follow Him even if forsaken of all men is the standard of discipleship, and if one is not thus willing to follow Him, he cannot be His disciple. This has been and can be done. Paul wrote to Timothy, "At my first answer no man stood with me, but all men forsook me . . . Notwithstanding the Lord stood with me, and strengthened me" (2 Tim. 4:16-17).

We are called upon to follow Him should all forsake us and death be our lot. Man can go no further. Paul and others did go that far—forsaken of all and accepting death, but not forsaken of God.

Here Jesus must go beyond; He must be forsaken by all and in death by God himself. Here the Christian need never go. He asks no one to follow Him here. In fact, He took this last step forsaken by God so that no one else need go that far. He paid the utmost farthing of sin's just penalty that I and all who will accept His pardon may go free. Such is the infinite salvation gained for man in His last hours alone: He went there alone that we need never be alone; He will be with us "alway."

There is another area into which the Christian cannot follow Him—the realm of total temptation. It was necessary for Him to experience every tempting power of Satan, and He was led of the Holy Spirit into that maelstrom of satanic deception and seductiveness. He knew that we should not follow Him that far, so He has taught us to pray the Father to "lead us not into temptation" (Matt. 6:13; Luke 11:4). That reverses the pattern of His guidance; we need not—should not—follow Him there.

I can view these two areas of His human life and feel no compunction of conscience when I say, "Jesus did; I don't." More than that, I am delighted not to follow Him here.

Having justified myself in not following Him here, I ask,

48

Am I justified in not following Him in other areas of His life? Where does the "Follow me not" sign end and the "Follow me" begin? Is His whole life a pattern for ours except when He announces exceptions? Is it here, as it was in the Garden of Eden, that all the fruit of His life is to be partaken of except the forbidden? Does the "Follow me" include all the rest?

There is a great segment of His life of which I must say in truth, "Jesus did; I don't"; and am I herein justified or condemned? The failure I confess, but is it commendable or condemnable? I speak of His prayer life. Let us look at it fairly. And whatever may be our obligation, either to follow Him or let Him go alone, I admit I do not follow Him here, or, at best, afar off.

When we examine His prayer life in the light of what is written and in full honesty, we must admit that Jesus made a large place in His life to be alone with the Father. The facts support such a conclusion. Here are some of them.

Take the case of the feeding of the 5,000 with the five loaves and the two fishes (Matt. 14:15-21). At the close of the day "he sent the multitudes away," and "he went up into a mountain apart to pray" (vv. 22-23). We find Him next between three and six the next morning, walking on the sea to protect the disciples from the ravages of the storm. The inference is that He had spent the night in prayer.

Mark gives an account of His "rising up a great while before day" and departing into a solitary place to pray (1:35).

Luke records "that he went out into a mountain to pray, and continued all night in prayer to God" (6:12).

John gives us a penetrating insight into His prayer life that leads us to believe that His mountain trysts were the customary and not unusual practices of the Master. Under pressure to accept kingship "he departed again into a mountain himself alone" (6:15). The "again" is significant. He had been there before; often and long were the hours He spent alone with the Father.

After the great catch of fish and other miracles "he withdrew himself into the wilderness, and prayed" (Luke 5:16).

It seems that He spent a full night on the Mount of Transfiguration, as it was "on the next day, when they were come down from the hill, much people met him" (9:37). Luke also records that "in the day time he was teaching in the temple; and at night he went out, and abode in the mount that is called the mount of Olives" (21:37).

That His long vigils of prayer were not the unusual, Luke's story (22:39) clearly reveals. He records, "And he came out, and went, as he was wont, to the mount of Olives." We gain a deeper insight here by using the different translations of the text, some of which are:

"He proceeded as usual to the Mount of Olives" (Weymouth).

"He came out, and went, as his custom was, unto the mount of Olives" (ASV).

"He went . . . up the Mount of Olives, as He was in the habit of doing" (Williams).

"He went . . . as he had often done before" (Phillips).

Viewing the record through the eyes of many Bible scholars confirms the fact that He spent much time alone with the Father in prayer.

One more reference will show Him in contrast with the rulers of the Pharisees. Secret service men had been sent out to entrap Him in His words and bring Him to trial, but had returned, saying, "Never man spake like this man." Nicodemus broke up the hearing by asking, "Doth our law judge any man, before it hear him, and know what he doeth?" Then follow two contrasting actions: "And every man went unto his own house. Jesus went unto the mount of Olives" (John 7:45—8:1). Others went to sleep or scheme or wrangle; Jesus went to pray.

The preponderance of evidence clearly establishes the fact that Jesus made a large place in His life to be alone with the Father. No biblical truth is better established and no habit of His life better supported by His teachings. He taught and practiced the art of prayer.

In the light of the facts in His prayer life and mine, I am forced to say, "Jesus Did; I Don't." I am not confessing that I do not pray—I do; I have been praying for about 72 years. But I certainly would lie should I profess to maintain a prayer life anything near comparable to His. The important question is, Should I? Was His pattern peculiar to Him alone and not to be followed by His children? Whatever answer I may give in word, the answer of my action is that I am not obliged to thus follow Him. Is this the correct answer, and with what facts may I support it?

Since the answer of my actions appears to be about the same as my fellows, I have been asking the question, Why do we not follow His prayer pattern? Certainly His was not sinful. And since we claim that we desire to be like Him, why the unlikeness here? Through the years I have circulated through some of the larger audiences to which I was ministering, a questionnaire containing two questions. The first: Is your prayer life satisfactory to yourself? Yes ( ) No ( ). Second, if the answer is "No," then why this unsatisfactory condition? About 90 percent answering the questions have said "No" to the first question; and about 85 percent of those answering "No" have, in one form or another, claimed that they were too busy to maintain the kind of prayer life that they felt they should have. Most felt that the Master's prayer life should be the pattern for us, but we are too busy to follow it.

At this point in the discussion I do not care to express my opinion on the matter, but I will bring before us another area of action of which I can and must, if honest, say, "Jesus Did; I Don't."

"He taught . . . as one having authority" (Matt. 7:29). I don't. The record sustains this appraisal of His authority. In contrast to His speaking, the scribes, Pharisees, and teachers

51

of the law in His day were versed in the "tradition of the elders." They could quote by the hour, but their message did not penetrate. They were "sounding brass"; no one was moved by them (1 Cor. 13:1). Jesus spoke, and they knew that they had heard from another world. Those who heard did not always agree as to the world heard from, but they acknowledged His message as being "out of this world." Some believed that it came from God, while some thought it came from Beelzebub, the prince of devils. It was not a merely human message. It had power, power to arouse the enmity of His enemies and the devotion of His would-be followers.

Now may I ask: Is there any connection between His prayer life and His speaking? Did the power in His message grow out of His oft vigils with the Father? I am assuming that every speaker of divine truth would like to have His power to proclaim it; and what if it be found that His praying and His power cannot be separated? Would we be willing to be devoid of His power rather than to adopt its source—aloneness with the Father?

Consider another area of His ministry: His supernatural works—healing, casting out devils, and such like. "Jesus Did; I Don't." These statements need no proof; the record is the Book, and proves Christ as a miracle worker. My record proves that I am not a miracle worker. Should I be? What shall be done with the Master's statement, "He that believeth on me, the works that I do shall he do also" (John 14:12)? Dare we face this one frankly? What about it?

Was there a connection between the works of His life and the pattern of His praying? And if the answer is yes, the question then is, Are we willing to forfeit the opportunity of doing His works rather than enter into the secret of His praying?

Again, it is said of Him, "He himself knew what he would do" (John 6:6). These words were spoken when He was faced with 5,000 hungry people and turned to Philip to inquire about the food supply. "This he said to prove him." He knew that Philip could not meet the emergency. He would not know where to buy, and besides that, he didn't have the money; but Jesus had the answer. Our Lord was never stumped by hard questions nor baffled by impossible situations. He always knew what to do; I don't. Here the gulf between us is wide. We struggle and are perplexed to find solutions. He had them in due time.

Jesus brought division; I don't. And the sad part is, I am not like Him. Jesus taught nothing more clearly than that His ministry and His kingdom were divisive. No teacher ever disturbed the status quo more than Jesus; that He admitted. He declared, "Think not that I am come to send peace on earth: I came not to send peace, but a sword. For I am come to set a man at variance against his father, and the daughter against her mother, and the daughter in law against her mother in law. And a man's foes shall be they of his own household. He that loveth father or mother more than me is not worthy of me: and he that loveth son or daughter more than me is not worthy of me. And he that taketh not his cross, and followeth after me, is not worthy of me. He that findeth his life shall lose it: and he that loseth his life for my sake shall find it" (Matt. 10:34-39). He reminded His followers, "If the world hate you, ye know that it hated me before it hated you. . . . If they have persecuted me, they will also persecute you" (John 15:18, 20).

Again He said, "Woe unto you, when all men shall speak well of you! for so did their fathers to the false prophets" (Luke 6:26). Such sentiments are not overly emphasized in our day, and in many instances virtually ignored. Paul's exhortation to Timothy that a bishop "must have a good report of them which are without" (1 Tim. 3:7), and his expressed desire "that ye might walk worthy of the Lord unto all pleasing" (Col. 1:10) are so glamorized that we often fail to remember that the same apostle spoke of his "persecutions and afflictions" that came to him, and reminded the same Timothy that "all that will live godly in Christ Jesus shall suffer persecution" (2 Tim. 3:12).

The spear-riven side of the Master and the severed head of the apostle but illustrate their teachings that the gospel message and the Christlike life produce suffering and may claim the lives of those thus following the Savior. Here again, I say they suffered greatly; I don't.

In thus contrasting myself with the Master, I would not infer that I do not follow Him, although I must admit that I follow afar off. Is the gap too wide? and if so, Why? I answer the first question with an unqualified yes. There is too much distance between me and Christ. The second question is Why? And then comes the third: How may this weakness be remedied? The answer to the third question is implicit in the answer to the second, Why?

Why have we allowed this wide gap to remain so wide? I do not claim to know the full answer, but I can give a major part of it: We have not allowed Jesus to be what the Word declares Him to be: "Jesus of Nazareth, a man" (Acts 2:22).

We have often conceived of Him as possessing all the qualities of the Infinite Father inherently: standing alone in His own strength, speaking His self-devised message, and possessing eternal life as an inherent quality and giving it to as many as He would. Thus standing in our vision as the Infinite calling us to follow Him, we reply, in action, if not in words, We can't, we are human; You are infinite. We are weak; You are all-powerful. We are ignorant; You are all-wise. Taunt us not with Your invitation. You have arrived; we are in the making. You have more than a head start. The distance between us is infinite. We find no footprints on the low path of our misfortune. Would we might have been born to power, wisdom, and self-sufficiency as were You! But, alas, we were not!

54

Too often this is our conception of Christ; He is remote, removed, and alone. Turning to Him for His appraisal of himself, we find quite another picture, the picture of a man "made in the likeness of men" (Phil. 2:7). "In all things it behoved him to be made like unto his brethren" (Heb. 2:17).

The Dependent Christ

Jesus was wholly dependent upon the Father. He affirmed, "I live by the Father" (John 6:57). To the devil He said, "Man shall not live by bread alone, but by every word that proceedeth out of the mouth of God" (Matt. 4:4).

He brought to earth no message of His own and performed no works of His own initiative. He made these facts very clear. His words are: "The Son can do nothing of himself, but what he seeth the Father do" (John 5:19). When He said "nothing," He meant nothing and reaffirmed it, saying, "I can of mine own self do nothing" (v. 30).

At first thought, these statements appear to reveal a weakness of the Son, but upon deeper thought they reveal His strength. Since He was utterly dependent upon the Father, He became a perfect channel through which the Father could perfectly work.

He presented no countercurrents of thought and offered no resistance of action. He moved only with the Father's movements and spoke only the Father's words. He revealed the secret of ultimate success—abandonment of self to God.

This perfect alignment with the Father was something that He acquired through practice. "Though he were a Son, yet learned he obedience by the things which he suffered" (Heb. 5:8). Here He set a perfect pattern for us. He never rebelled. His submission was constant and complete.

Christ bore no responsibility for initiating what He said or what He did. He denied saying anything of himself. Said He, "The word which ye hear is not mine, but the Father's which sent me" (John 14:24). Again, He affirmed, "As my Father hath taught me, I speak these things" (8:28).

Speaking only the Father's words, He had the backing of the Almighty and therefore spoke with authority. Likewise, He had no responsibility for what He said, for the Father bore this responsibility.

What was true of His words was true also of His works. He said, "I do nothing of myself" (John 8:28). Again, "The Father that dwelleth in me, he doeth the works" (14:10). He was absolutely helpless; He made himself so by His complete abandonment to God. This made it possible for the Father to reveal himself to men perfectly; therefore, Jesus could say, "He that hath seen me hath seen the Father" (v. 9). His every movement was that of the Father, and this left Him free and irresponsible—responsible only for His total abandonment to God.

Because of His total commitment to God and utter inability to do anything except what He saw His Father do, it was safe for the Father to show Him what He was doing. Because of this, Jesus could say, "The Father loveth the Son, and sheweth him all things that himself doeth" (John 5:20).

Jesus was conscious of His helplessness, else He would not have told us of it. He knew also that this sense of dependence upon God and loyalty to Him opened the way for His Father to speak and work through Him perfectly. His helplessness opened the door for the Father's strength.

Can there be any practical value in the exploration of Christ's life pattern unless it presents a way of life for us? Is His life relevant? May the pattern of His life become contemporary?

It appears that the apostle Paul caught something of the practical meaning of the Master's weakness when he said, "When I am weak, then am I strong" (2 Cor. 12:10). He was realizing that to be emptied of self was to present to the Fa-

57

ther a usable vessel, and this is the message that we sorely need to learn.

It is only as we understand Christ's helplessness that we can understand the wisdom of His hiding away in olive groves and the mountains to be alone with His Father. He said He learned of Him, and learning takes time. He could do only those things that He saw His Father doing, and it takes time to see.

Jesus not only claimed to be dependent upon the Father, but He acted like it. He did not shun His schooling although at times it required the whole night. He never went into the arena of action without first seeing and hearing; hence, His wisdom, His power and authority. He presented the empty vessel for the filling, and the Father failed Him not.

We are enjoined to "let this mind be in you, which was also in Christ Jesus" (Phil. 2:5). The apostle explains what he means, and a major in that explanation is that "he emptied himself" (v. 7, margin). This was the secret of the Master's power and success: He prepared himself for Another's filling. One of life's most difficult tasks is to empty oneself of self. We think of emptying out self-seeking, self-centered desire, self-ishness, and various other things, but self itself must be yielded. The soul must first become empty before it can be filled with Another. In some such manner, Christ emptied himself. His will He negated. He accepted the Father's as His own. We are asked to do the same.

It is reasonable to believe that if one empties himself and offers the empty vessel to God for the using, that God will take charge and use the vessel. It is the presence of self that hinders: self asserting itself, self vocal and vibrant, self holding the veto power—in short, self still ruler.

Jesus represents the perfect emptying and the perfect filling. The waters that flowed from His soul bore no sediment of self. It was God, fresh and life-giving.

Jesus never claimed to possess what He did not have. He

58

had nothing and did not hesitate to say so. He not only admitted His utter dependence upon the Father but acknowledged that all that He had came from the Father. What He had, He inherited from God, and the sole purpose of His life was to obey, please, and bring honor to Him from whom He had received all that He had—even life itself.

It must be that God is looking to find someone to walk in the footsteps of His Son, claiming no power of His own but relying fully on the Father for all. It is not that God has no power to impart to men, but it is that there are few, if any, fully prepared to receive it and use it for Him. Christ did and led the way for us.

Jesus Would Not Follow Jesus, Thank God!

At first sight, the title of this chapter may not receive a favorable response, and to add the "thank God" may only serve to alienate the casual thinker. I would, therefore, ask for an open-minded reading, and I am convinced that, thus reading, one will share with me the same viewpoint, for this is the viewpoint of the Master.

Of old it was prophesied of Him, "Then said I, Lo, I come: in the volume of the book it is written of me, I delight to do thy will, O my God" (Ps. 40:7-8). Under divine inspiration, the writer of the Hebrews uses this prophecy thus: "Then said I, Lo, I come (in the volume of the book it is written of me,) to do thy will, O God" (10:7).

When Jesus came to earth, He repeatedly reaffirmed this purpose of obedience to the Father. His words are: "My meat is to do the will of him that sent me" (John 4:34). "I seek . . . the will of the Father which hath sent me" (5:30). "I came down from heaven . . . to do . . . the will of him that sent me" (6:38). If one should take these statements alone, he might conclude that Jesus and the Father were so indivisibly one and their wills so inseparable that the doing of the Father's will by Jesus was necessarily inevitable.

Was the will of the Father and the will of Jesus one and the same? Must they stand or fall together? Could there have been a parting of the way? Were this "Jesus of Nazareth, a man" (Acts 2:22), spoken of by Peter on the Day of Pentecost, and the "God [that] was in Christ" (2 Cor. 5:19), about which the apostle Paul wrote, inseparably connected? May we speak of the "will of God" and the "will of Jesus" interchangeably and refer to the same thing always? In short, were they identical?

Before answering these questions, one must complete the half-quoted statements of Jesus mentioned above. To complete them, we must add: "I seek not mine own will" (John 5:30). "I came down from heaven, not to do mine own will" (6:38). In that dark hour of Gethsemane, His final prayer was "Not as I will, but as thou wilt" (Matt. 26:39). By His own words, He did not follow himself. If His will and the Father's were identical, then when He was saying no to His own will, He was at the same time saying no to the will of the Father. Jesus clearly brought out the contrast between His will and the Father's when He said, "Not my will, but thine, be done" (Luke 22:42). One cannot say yes and no to the same thing at the same time. To the one will, Jesus said no; to the other, He said yes. They could, therefore, be neither the same nor necessarily alike.

What clearer proof than this do we need that *Jesus did not follow Jesus?* He followed the Father, not Jesus. It was not safe for Him to follow himself. If so, why did He say no to himself? Jesus never relied on the God that He was, but always on His Father who was in heaven.

There is still further proof that Jesus did not rely upon Jesus. He said, "If I bear witness of myself, my witness is not true" (John 5:31). Here He was saying that His testimony was not true just because He was giving it, but it was true because it was but an echo of the testimony given by the Father. "There is another that beareth witness of me; and I know that the witness which he witnesseth of me is true" (v. 32).

At a later date, Jesus was making the claim that He was the Light of the World. The Jews who had heard of His former statement challenged Him and accused Him of telling

61

an untruth because He was testifying of himself. He defended what He was saying as being the truth, not because He said it, but because "the Father that sent me beareth witness of me" (cf. John 8:12-18).

Jesus never tried to establish His ministry on an inherent Godhood but upon the attestation of supernatural proofs that His ministry was of the Father. The reoccurring Voice from above and the "works which none other man did" (John 15:24) were the pillars for faith in Him and not the claims that He made of himself. He did not demand obedience to His message because He was delivering it, but because the message was not His own. "The word which ye hear is not mine, but the Father's which sent me" (14:24). The very fact that it was not His own but the Father's made it binding.

Jesus insisted upon the justice of His judgment, not because it was His. "And yet if I judge, my judgment is true: for I am not alone, but I and the Father that sent me" (8:16). In fact, He was saying, My judgment is just because it is not Mine; there is finality in what I am saying only because I am speaking the words of My Father, and His words, and His alone, are final.

Jesus did make some claims for himself such as: "I am the light of the world"; "I am the resurrection, and the life"; "the words that I speak unto you . . . are life" (John 8:12; 11:25; 6:63). These and other claims He did make of himself, but He reminded us that these claims are true not because He made them, but because of the words and acts of the Father. He could boldly say, "The words that I speak unto you . . . are life" because He had affirmed that "the word which ye hear is not mine, but the Father's which sent me" (14:24).

He did say, "I am . . . the life," but He also explained that this life was not inherently His but that it had come from the "Father of lights" (James 1:17) as a gift. "For as the Father hath life in himself; so hath he given to the Son to have life in himself" (John 5:26). It was inherent in the Father but given in the Son. He did say, "I am the light of the world," but He had explained that that light was not inherently His but that it was an emanation from life that had been imparted to Him by the Father. This explanation had already been given: "In him was life; and the life was the light of men" (1:4). Light and life are inseparable.

Not only did life, light, and His words come from the Father, but all that He possessed had, in like manner, come from the Father. He denied any strength of His own, saying, "I can of mine own self do nothing" (John 5:30), but relied upon His Father of whom He said, "My Father is greater than I" (14:28).

In the 25th chapter of Matthew, Jesus pictured himself as the Judge of the universe, dividing the sheep from the goats and saying to the sheep, "Come, ye blessed of my Father, inherit the kingdom prepared for you from the foundation of the world" (v. 34). To the goats He said, "Depart from me, ye cursed, into everlasting fire, prepared for the devil and his angels" (v. 41). This position was not inherently His. He got it from Another. Jesus said, "For the Father judgeth no man, but hath committed all judgment unto the Son" (John 5:22). Peter confirms this: "And he [Christ] commanded us to preach unto the people, and to testify that it is he which was ordained of God to be the Judge of quick and dead" (Acts 10:42). Paul adds this confirmation, "Because he [God] hath appointed a day, in the which he will judge the world in righteousness by that man whom he hath ordained; whereof he hath given assurance unto all men, in that he hath raised him from the dead" (17:31).

Note that His Judgeship had been "committed" to him by the Father. Note also that the Father had "ordained" Him as Judge, affirmed by both Peter and Paul. More especially, it should be noted that this ordination as Judge was not made to Him because He was the Son of God, for Jesus said, "And hath given him authority to execute judgment also, because he is the Son of man" (John 5:27).

It is noteworthy also that the throne that Jesus is to occupy was not His inherently, but "the Lord God shall give unto him the throne of his father David" (Luke 1:32).

Examine His whole portfolio and you will find that what was His had been committed to Him by God. Such was not His by virtue of an inherent Godhood, but by the sovereignty of the Almighty Father. Just look at the list and note the source of them: His priesthood, Saviorhood, Heirship, and inheritance; His resurrection, power, followers, things, glory, and authority to rule the nations "with a rod of iron"—all of these and doubtless more came from Another. He did not come into the world Possessor of all these things. Many of them came to Him as rewards, or as we might say, prizes for services well rendered, battles well fought, and a godlike spirit. The following may be used as illustrating this fact: "Thou hast loved righteousness, and hated iniquity; therefore God, even thy God, hath anointed thee with the oil of gladness above thy fellows" (Heb. 1:9). Note the "therefore." The anointing was a reward for His godlike attitude toward iniquity and righteousness.

In one of Paul's penetrating insights into Christ's preincarnate glory and subsequent emptying, he pictures Him as "being in the form of God" but voluntarily emptying himself, taking the form of a servant and becoming "obedient unto death, even the death of the cross." The apostle then announces His exaltation: "Wherefore God also hath highly exalted him, and given him a name which is above every name" (see Phil. 2:5-11). Note the "wherefore." It is pointing out the reason for the exaltation. It was a prize He had won by the "mind" that was in Him.

This truth is further illustrated by the fact that the seat now occupied with the Father is a seat that was won by overcoming. A seat by His side in His throne is offered as a reward to us for overcoming. That is the way He won the high seat, and by the same method, His followers may win a seat with Him. Such a seat with Christ is not inherently ours but must be won at a price. The same was true of Him. It was not His by virtue of His Sonship but came as a reward (see Rev. 3:21).

While on earth Christ was a Savior in the making. He developed into Saviorhood. Absolute and perfect and constant obedience was required of Him if He was to fulfill the law. The spirit of obedience was always His, even unto death, but the application of that spirit to life's situations was an accomplishment to be attained by the suffering processes of life. Hence it is written of Him, "Though he were a Son, yet learned he obedience by the things which he suffered" (Heb. 5:8). If it was something that He must learn, it is evident that He did not possess it in its fullest until after He had suffered. One cannot learn what he already knows.

After His resurrection and the outpouring of the Holy Ghost on the Day of Pentecost, Peter declared, "God hath made that same Jesus . . . both Lord and Christ" (Acts 2:36). He was not, at first, perfect enough to qualify as Savior. The writer of Hebrews reminds us that if the Captain of our salvation is to bring many sons unto glory, He must be made perfect through sufferings. These necessary sufferings were not all accomplished in His lifetime. They extended through death; for as a part of redemption's plan, the devil had to be destroyed, and he could only be destroyed through the death of our Captain. We are told that Christ partook of death "that through death he might destroy him that had the power of death, that is, the devil" (Heb. 2:14).

As Jesus journeyed along the road of full obedience, He had the repeated approval of the Father. As He began His ministry in baptism, "the heavens were opened unto him . . . and lo a voice from heaven, saying, This is my beloved Son, in whom I am well pleased" (Matt. 3:16-17). On the Mount of

65

Transfiguration "a voice out of the cloud . . . said, This is my beloved Son, in whom I am well pleased" (17:5). Near the end of His life, He prayed, "Father, glorify thy name. Then came there a voice from heaven, saying, I have both glorified it, and will glorify it again" (John 12:28). Here He was facing His last days, and in this connection, He had said, "Therefore doth my Father love me, because I lay down my life, that I might take it again" (10:17).

The Father forsook Him in death. He was not in some irresponsible delirium when He cried out, "My God, my God, why hast thou forsaken me?" (Matt. 27:46; Mark 15:34). Nevertheless, the cause of the rejection was atoned for by His death, and then the Father vindicated Him and accepted His sacrifice and gave evidence of His continued approval by raising Him from the dead and seating Him at His own right hand in heaven.

Regardless of all the repeated approvals given to Him as He journeyed this road of total obedience, they all would be meaningless insofar as the sinners of all ages are concerned, if He had not received this approval upon His death; for His death was to atone for our sins, and the approval of His atoning death set divine approval upon the efficacy of man's redemption through the blood of Christ.

All that Jesus ever did or said while on earth—even His death upon the Cross—would have no saving benefit for any human creature from Adam to the last born child of woman if the story had ended there. Paul sets this forth in plain and graphic manner in the 15th chapter of 1 Corinthians, and it need not be enlarged upon here. A reading of Paul's statement at this point would be rewarding indeed.

The Resurrection at the tomb would never have been possible without the death upon the Cross; hence, we sing with the great apostle, "But God forbid that I should glory, save in the cross of our Lord Jesus Christ" (Gal. 6:14). He knew that there could be no resurrection without a death. He gloried in the death because it was suffered in our stead and was an indispensable prerequisite to a resurrection, without which our redemption was impossible. While we glory in the Cross, we shout at the empty tomb. At the Cross He "was delivered for our offences," while at the tomb He "was raised again for our justification" (Rom. 4:25). There could have been a death without a resurrection, but there could not be a resurrection without a death; and the Resurrection is the signal of our salvation—hence, the place of our rejoicing. Our salvation is a death-life process. Death is the portal; life is the palace.

There is a still deeper sense in which Jesus does not ask us to accept His saying as final, but cites us to the higher promise of the Father and then to its fulfillment. Jesus promised to send the Holy Spirit upon His followers. These promises are concise: "If I go not away, the Comforter will not come unto you; but if I depart, I will send him unto you" (John 16:7). This is a definite promise of Jesus. Another equally clear is, "But when the Comforter is come, whom I will send unto you from the Father" (15:26).

In this connection Jesus announced the effectiveness of His prayers: "And I will pray the Father, and he shall give you another Comforter" (John 14:16). He further refers to "the Comforter, which is the Holy Ghost, whom the Father will send in my name" (v. 26). The answer to His prayer is thus announced, "Therefore being by the right hand of God exalted, and having received of the Father the promise of the Holy Ghost, he hath shed forth this, which ye now see and hear" (Acts 2:33). He appeals to what the Father said: "I send the promise of my Father upon you" (Luke 24:49). "And . . . commanded them [to] wait for the promise of the Father, which, saith he, ye have heard of me" (Acts 1:4).

In these statements of Jesus concerning the coming of the Holy Ghost and their fulfillment, four important facts occurred.

First: Jesus claimed to have power with God in prayer, and facts that followed proved it.

Second: He claimed to have had a specific promise from the Father. Facts proved this also.

Third: He pinpointed the time of the fulfillment of the promise, and they were to wait for it.

Fourth: His oneness with the Father was such that their action in sending the Holy Spirit was a joint action: "The Father will send"; "I will send."

To round out the promises of the Holy Spirit's coming, we should add the wider promise made by Peter on the Day of Pentecost: "For the promise is unto you, and to your children, and to all that are afar off, even as many as the Lord our God shall call" (Acts 2:39).

Paul declared that if Christ had not been raised from the dead, all who had trusted in Him perished. In the same vein of truth, it may be said that if the Holy Ghost had not been sent on His waiting followers at Pentecost, and if He is not available to His followers today, then all that preceded it was in vain.

To state the matter from my own personal viewpoint, I say, If Jesus did not make available the Holy Spirit for His disciples at Pentecost, and if He is not available to believers today, then I am not interested in any of the promises Jesus made while upon earth. These comforting promises, "Let not your heart be troubled: ye believe in God, believe also in me. . . . I go to prepare a place for you. . . . I will come again, and receive you . . . where I am, there ye may be also" (John 14:1-3); "Whosoever believeth in me shall never die" (11:26); and "I am the way" (14:6), and all other such glowing promises would mean nothing to me without Pentecost. If He made clear, definite, and repeated promises of the Holy Spirit, and because of His untruthfulness or inability to fulfill these promises they were not fulfilled, why should I be interested in anything else that He promised?

Whatever glory we have given to His matchless life, His far-reaching promises, and His vicarious death, that glory must fade away if there were no Pentecost for the disciples and none available to us today. The coming of the Holy Spirit was for the disciples, and is for us today. Pentecost is the climactic and absolutely indispensable proof of His Saviorhood. Blot out the possibility of the Holy Spirit's coming, and with that felled stroke every foundation pillar of hope for immortality will have been annihilated.

The coming of the Holy Spirit is the coming of the living God, and without the living God we have no God that can give life. His coming is the final and conclusive proof that all that Jesus said of himself, of the Father, and of us is true. He can be accepted as God, for God the Father has validated all of His claims and has placed all things in His hands.

In the coming of the Holy Spirit, we have the witness that Christ is true, and it is upon His witness that our salvation stands. The Holy Ghost's coming is the beacon light casting its silvery beams back across the life, the words, and the deeds of the Master, bringing into focus the whole of His earthly and heavenly ministry with the perfect will of God. The oneness of the Father and the Son is clearly revealed, and time has validated the words of the Master, "I do always those things that please him" (John 8:29).

Father, Glorify Thy Name

(John 12:28)

The words of this theme were spoken by Jesus in one of His most trying hours. The context gives the full story and should be read. This was His final request on this occasion and represents His deepest desire. His whole life gives testimony to this fact.

However, it is interesting to know that His first request was of a different nature. It represents a human desire: "Father, save me from this hour." When He weighed His personal desire against the purpose of His Father's will, He brought His personal desire in line with that will.

This is the second time Jesus made a transition in His prayer from an expressed desire of His own to an acceptance of the Father's will. It was in Gethsemane that He prayed, Father . . . take away this cup from me" (Mark 14:36). Both requests were made in hours of intense suffering and imminent death. They reveal the human nature of the Son and also His firm purpose to do the Father's will. He had come to earth for that purpose and never changed that purpose. When any expressed desires, as in these two cases, were found to be out of harmony with the will of the Father, He changed His request.

It is in moments such as these that He revealed a normal humanity and showed His kinship with us. Were there no human traits ever to appear in the Master, we would have no

70

courage to follow Him; but this reminds us that He was "made like unto his brethren" (Heb. 2:17), and yet He could and did fulfill the Father's will. He did not do so by an infinite selfhood but by a suffering sainthood. In such hours, He was learning "obedience by the things which he suffered" (5:8). Being like His brethren, He could learn in no other way, but He learned and obeyed.

We thank God that He wore no halo to hide His face of sorrow. We see the Man that He was, and that we can and ought to be, shining through the clouds of suffering and of sorrow. He wore no smile in the garden and gave no shout at the approach of the traitor; He was "a man of sorrows, and acquainted with grief" (Isa. 53:3). We know that He can understand our sufferings, for we see the evidence in His marred face.

Too often has the glory of His exaltation concealed the shame of His rejection. Beholding Him on His heavenly throne, one might easily forget that He once wore a crown of thorns and bore a heavy cross. If we can see Him only in His present majesty, we could lose Him from the paths of time and find ourselves with a remote deity and not a traveling Companion.

It is well that the "man Christ Jesus," perfectly human and wholly dependent upon His Heavenly Father, be kept in focus lest we come to feel that He does not know and understand.

It is in such moments as are reflected in our theme that we can see One of our own nature reaching for an easier way out, but always accepting the Father's will. It is recorded that "he pleased not himself" (Rom. 15:3), but He also records, "I do always those things that please him" (John 8:29). There must be a reason for His exaltation, and that reason is His voluntary condescension and obedience unto death.

While it is true that by looking at the exalted Christ we are inspired to follow in His train, it is equally true that if He left no certain tracks in the sands of our sorrows, we could not find our way to a seat beside Him.

The glory of Christ was not that God was in Him, although that was true, but that the indwelling God did not destroy His weakness and leave Him without the need of angels' care. We can understand and join Him on life's lowly road and know that while walking it, He made plain the path to His eternal glory.

I glory in His expressions of personal desires. They strike a kindred chord, and I glory also that He did not rest in self-desire but moved to the unshakable purposes of the Father's will. It inspires me to follow along His path.

To me, His glory was that He was one with us—no distant God whose awesome visage forbids our coming, but a scarred hand and a broken heart where hopeless souls may find love and brotherhood. He is not ashamed to call us brethren because He was homeless and forsaken. He welcomed us in a common poverty and beckons us upward to a palace in the sky.

The very thought of Christ thrills my soul. I can approach Him without an introduction, eat with Him without a tuxedo, and feel no shame because of my poverty and rags.

He is one among us, not demanding the seat of honor, but donning the garments of a servant. No peasant is too lowly to be welcomed into His company, and no scarlet woman too vile to get His "go, and sin no more" (John 8:11).

Within himself He was weak, but in His Father He had all power; and following the pattern of His trust, we too can have access to the resources that were available to Him.

If He had come to earth in the majesty of His preincarnate glory, we would have despaired of attaining to His companionship; but He came as a helpless babe and struggled to perfection by the way of suffering and shame. And the path He trod can be trodden by us; the Cross that He bore can be shared by us; and the throne that He obtained can be shared by us also.

He did not soar above us but landed on our runway and with an open door invites us to enter; and thus entering, our flight to realms of splendor and of joy is assured. Blessed be His name—my Lord and Savior, Jesus Christ!

The Father Could Not Redeem Us

To say that God the Father—the Infinite—could not redeem the human race is, at first, shocking; and yet it is true. The price of redemption was blood, "for it is the blood that maketh an atonement for the soul" (Lev. 17:11); and "without shedding of blood is no remission" (Heb. 9:22). Jesus said, "God is a Spirit" (John 4:24), and "a spirit hath not flesh and bones" (Luke 24:39). And yet He said, "Except ye eat the flesh of the Son of man, and drink his blood, ye have no life in you" (John 6:53). It follows that the Incarnation—Christ's becoming flesh and blood—was an absolute necessity in the scheme of man's redemption.

The emphasis in redemption is on the man. "By one man sin entered into the world," and "righteousness shall reign . . . by one, [the Man] Jesus Christ" (Rom. 5:12, 17). The "first man Adam" wrecked us; the "last Adam" came to redeem us. Paul tells us, "The first man is of the earth, earthy: the second man is the Lord from heaven" (1 Cor. 15:45, 47).

Sin came by man, and redemption must come by man—the sinless Man. Furthermore, that Man from above—the only begotten Son of God—must be of Adam's race, and like others of that race (except sin). And He was just that. "In all things it behoved him to be made like unto his brethren" (Heb. 2:17), so that He could be "in all points tempted like as we are" (4:15).

74

Having taken on him "the seed of Abraham" (2:16), He was in a position to acquire an experiential knowledge of man that He did not have in His preincarnate state, and this newly acquired knowledge was necessary to qualify Him as man's Redeemer.

Now that it is clear that the Father has made Christ to be the Savior of our souls, it comes as a great relief; for the mind staggers and could break in its effort to understand a God who is spirit—one whom "no man hath seen . . . at any time" (1 John 4:12), for He dwelleth "in the light which no man can approach unto; whom no man hath seen, nor can see" (1 Tim. 6:16). This fact is reaffirmed in John's Gospel: "No man hath seen God at any time" (1:18).

It is a relief to know that my Savior is approachable. He came in the flesh, He ate, He slept, He sorrowed, He loved, and He revealed himself to us.

But what about the Father—the Sovereign of the universe of whom Paul said, "To us there is but one God, the Father, of whom are all things" (1 Cor. 8:6)? Have we no connection with Him who is supreme? The answer is yes. Jesus assures us that "he that loveth me shall be loved of my Father" (John 14:21). The goodwill of the Father is vouchsafed to us by the Son, and we have full assurance that the Son is in good rapport with the Father. His resurrection and seating at the Father's right hand are two of the many proofs of that.

Our task becomes more simple, our search less difficult. We need not try to penetrate the abode of the Infinite nor tax our minds with the impossible. We need only acquaint ourselves with the Man Christ Jesus. He wore the garments of clay, as do we. He fell upon death as must we. He sat on the well curb, spoke in the synagogue, ate at the homes of His friends, and conversed with all classes of people. In short, He was one of us.

We need not strain our feeble selves to try to compre-

75

hend His preincarnate nature or His heavenly abode. We need only know the Man of Galilee. He is approachable and easy to get acquainted with. In fact, He is calling all unto himself.

We are not charged with the hopeless task of trying to explore His nature, His past, and His eternal future. He has taken the responsibility of revealing himself to us, and that He is well able to do. The only catch here is that He has promised that self-revelation on conditions—the condition that we keep His commandments. The revelation is certain if the conditions are met; and if the revelation is not forthcoming, it is because the obedience is not forthcoming.

To those who hunger to know Him, here is the door— the door of obedience. We are often and solemnly warned to check our obedience. Many, the Master has told us, will be disappointed in the end because they have failed in obedience. We should check our conduct against His commandments and see just where we are.

The Sermon on the Mount is a good place to begin. He definitely states that those who disobey build on the sand, and their building will be swept away.

If anyone complains that the rules set forth by Him are too severe, it should be remembered that they have been tested by His own obedience. He has tried them all, and they are practical. He does not ask us to go where He has not gone. He is the Good Shepherd who, having put His sheep out, goeth before them. His tracks mark the way, and the way is the way of life.

While the Father could not redeem us, He sent His Son to do so, and He has accepted the redemption that His Son has provided. There is no question about the Father's attitude. He will not intervene in the final decisions, for He "hath committed all judgment unto the Son" (John 5:22). No one needs to move on to the judgment in doubt, for the decision of the Judge is available before the trial. "God hath sent forth the Spirit of his Son [the Judge] into your hearts, crying, Abba, Father" (Gal. 4:6).

There is nothing left to uncertainty. We may be sure, for His Spirit bears "witness with our spirit" as to our redemption (Rom. 8:16).

It is a thrill to know that we are dealing with a man—not an angel—but a man who "in all points" is like us; we can understand His message, for He speaks our language, and He has promised not to forsake us.

Viewed in this light, redemption for us seems so simple. It has been thus announced, so simple that "the wayfaring men, though fools, shall not err therein" (Isa. 35:8).

We may stand in awe of the palace, but the door is within our view; and entering in by the Door, we are promised life. Christ has come to make our salvation possible, and not only possible, but simple—so simple that a child may obtain it.

Although the Father could not redeem us, we praise Him that He begot a Son who can, and sent Him into the world for that purpose. We can't fathom it, but we can enjoy it, and be grateful.

The Third Day I Shall Be Perfected

(Luke 13:32)

The words of this text were spoken by Jesus to the Pharisees in answer to their reminder that Herod would kill Him. He declared, "I do cures to day and to morrow, and the third day I shall be perfected."

Jesus was dealing with the same matter earlier when He stated, "I have a baptism to be baptized with; and how am I straitened till it be accomplished!" (Luke 12:50).

He needed a perfection that He did not have at that time and could only acquire through suffering; and the climactic experience of that necessary suffering was death, separation from God, and suffering in hell. He knew it must be, and was "straitened till it be accomplished."

The writer of Hebrews tells us that "it became him . . . in bringing many sons unto glory, to make the captain of their salvation perfect through sufferings" (2:10). To complete the redemptive process, He must destroy the devil, and He could do that only by His own death. The record is clear that since "the children are partakers of flesh and blood, he . . . took part of the same; that through death he might destroy him that had the power of death, that is, the devil" (v. 14).

Jesus was constantly looking forward to His day of glorification—the day of His death—when He could prove His perfect obedience to the Father, even death upon the Cross in

78

sinful man's stead and its consequent rejection by God, and tasting death, eternal death, for man's sin.

He was teaching this truth to His disciples in this truism: "Except a corn of wheat fall into the ground and die, it abideth alone" (John 12:24). He was that corn of wheat and was looking forward to its being planted in death, that it might later bring forth much fruit, and He was "straitened till it be accomplished."

When the Greeks—the last flock of the lost sheep—sought Him, He faced the same issue: "Now is my soul troubled; and what shall I say? Father, save me from this hour: but for this cause came I unto this hour" (John 12:27). He then asked that the Father be glorified. He knew that the glorifying of the Father was linked with His own glorification. He had just finished stating, "The hour is come, that the Son of man should be glorified" (v. 23). Later He prayed, "Father, the hour is come; glorify thy Son, that thy Son also may glorify thee" (17:1).

On the third day, He was to be received by the Father if His death was acceptable to God; and as the high priest entered the holiest of all with blood, and must first be accepted before he could forgive the sins of the assembled people, so our High Priest must enter the holiest—even heaven itself—and have His sacrifice approved. Mary met Him when He was in process and before He ascended, and He told her, "Touch me not; for I am not yet ascended to my Father . . . and your Father" (John 20:17). After ascending, He allowed them to hold Him by the feet. He had been accepted in His final act of obedience and was now perfected on this third day.

When Abraham obeyed God, even to the proposed killing of his son (although it was not actual, it was spiritually real), God assured him, "Now I know that thou fearest God" (Gen. 22:12). Likewise, when Jesus gave the supreme obedience, He gained that perfection that a redeemer needed, "and being made perfect, he became the author of eternal salvation unto all them that obey him" (Heb. 5:9).

When one examines the record of the Master's life, he finds that Jesus walked this path of absolute obedience to the law of God, which culminated in this absolute perfection that was His glorification and qualification for Saviorhood. His first recorded step in this direction was when He was 12 in the Temple with the doctors of divinity, "both hearing them, and asking them questions" (Luke 2:46). When His parents found Him, He returned with them "and was subject unto them" (v. 51).

His total dedication to God demanded His obedience to His parents. In mature life, He was led by the Holy Spirit. He did not follow the leadership of men but that of His Father. He could say, "I do always those things that please him" (John 8:29). Having followed this line of obedience and finding himself always in the love of God, He commended it to us, saying, "If ye keep my commandments, ye shall abide in my love; even as I have kept my Father's commandments, and abide in his love" (15:10).

All along life's highway, it was His purpose to do the Father's will: "I came down from heaven, not to do mine own will, but the will of him that sent me" (6:38).

In His sorest struggle, His word was the same: "Not my will, but thine, be done" (Luke 22:42). Nothing short of absolute obedience would result in godlikeness, and nothing short of godlikeness would be perfection. Obedience, therefore, was the foundation stone of Jesus' career.

It is interesting to note that obedience had to be "learned" by Him: "Though he were a Son, yet learned he obedience by the things which he suffered" (Heb. 5:8). He learned by obedience, which is the indispensable prerequisite to understanding God's will. He preached this to others and practiced it himself. He was not perfect as the Redeemer of men until His suffering was complete; hence, the commandment that perfection would be reached on the third day—the day that His Father would raise Him from the dead and receive Him into heaven in proof of His perfect and total obedience.

It was this total obedience that qualified Him for Saviorhood, and salvation is offered to us only on the condition of obedience to Him—"unto all them that obey him" (Heb. 5:9).

There was no substitute for obedience for the Savior; and equally true, there is no salvation for us on any terms except total obedience to Him.

The record is, "For both he that sanctifieth and they who are sanctified are all of one: for which cause he is not ashamed to call them brethren" (Heb. 2:11). This oneness must be in obedience, and that unto death—always real and, at times, actual.

Salvation is promised only to those who obey Him. The disobedient will not be saved. The Christian's undivided purpose must be, like the Master's, to fully obey God. Thus purposing, he must follow the same suffering process to learn how to obey, that was followed by the Master. We can learn by no other. His became necessary because of us. We could learn in no other way, and He became like us and led the way to show us the path. Following Him, we will live with Him eternally.

Perfection was His when He had gone the last step in obedience; and for us, eternal salvation awaits us if we "endure unto the end" (Matt. 24:13).